INDIAN PICTURE WRITING

INDIAN PICTURE WRITING

WRITTEN AND ILLUSTRATED BY

ROBERT HOFSINDE

(GRAY-WOLF)

WILLIAM MORROW & COMPANY
New York   1959

TO

Library of Congress Catalog Card Number 59-6169

13   14   15   75

Contents

1. Indian Picture Writing

*Picture writing is a way of expressing thoughts and recording
events by marks or drawings. Cave men carved or painted scenes
of their hunts and exploits upon the walls of their dwellings.
The Egyptians recorded their deeds in paintings and in hiero-
glyphs, and the vikings carved theirs on stones. The American
Indians used picture writing to depict their legends and dreams,
personal triumphs in the hunt and on the battlefield, and family
and tribal history.*

Some of these drawings are crude in design; others are small masterpieces of primitive art. Many of them were painted red, green, yellow, and blue. The Indians made these colors from earth, grasses, plants, and flowers, which they dried, crushed into powder, and mixed with water. The colors were applied with brushes made of pieces of porous buffalo bone.

In the northern part of the United States, Indian picture writing is found on totem poles, wall paintings, and storage boxes. The Plains Indians of the North and West drew on hides or skins, and the Iroquois carved on posts and painted on the inner walls of their bark houses. Among the Woodland Indians, records of rituals and songs were frequently made on strips of birch bark and used to conduct ceremonies.

The Indians often painted themselves and their horses before riding into battle. These picture-writing symbols described past victories and were intended to frighten the enemy. Returning home after a successful war expedition, the warriors would halt and paint records of their deeds upon themselves and their horses before riding proudly into the village. Some of these markings and their meanings are given on page 88, and the illustration on page 89 shows how these markings were actually used.

In picture writing, many objects are indicated simply by drawing them. For example, the symbol of a dog is a picture of a dog. Other symbols are more abstract, but they are not difficult to understand. The word peace *is pictured as a broken arrow, for of course no one could fight with such a weapon.*

On the following pages you will see 248 pictures taken from

the Indians' picture writing. Some are old; others have been adapted for modern use. As you use these pictures, you may wish to add other symbols to represent things in the modern world.

Many of the drawings stand for more than one word. Two or more drawings can sometimes be combined to form still other words. Pictures that represent verbs can refer to past, present, or future actions.

Indian picture writing can be used to write letters to friends or to record camp or scouting events. A sample letter is shown on page 82, and on page 83 you will find the correct translation, first in the key number of each picture, then in English. Other sample letters are given on pages 84 to 86. If you have trouble with the translations, the answers are on pages 93 to 95.

For recording group events, use a small animal skin, as the Indians did. Water colors or waterproof India inks are best for this work. If you use paint, apply it with a small brush. The ink should be applied with a not-too-pointed pen. Since it is hard to correct a mistake on a skin, do your drawings on paper first and make certain they are right before drawing them on the skin.

Some skins are painted from left to right; others are painted in a spiral fashion, starting at the upper left corner and ending in the center of the skin. A skin with the spiral type of picture writing is shown on page 87, and a translation is given on page 96.

It is easy to develop skill in the art of picture writing, and boys and girls today can have fun using it for secret messages. By studying the symbols and the sample letters, you will soon be able to read and write in the Indian way.

GRAY·WOLF.

11

2. Picture-Writing Symbols

1. MAN (MALE, BOY)

2. **WOMAN (FEMALE, GIRL)** The dress, represented by the lower triangle, changes the figure from a man to a woman.

3. **BROTHERS** The two lines below the figures show that they come from the same family. They are holding hands, showing that they are directly related.

4. **SISTERS** Same as above, but here the figures are female.

5. **FRIENDS** Same as Brothers, but here there are no base lines.

6. **FATHER** When more than one figure appears, the shaded figure is the one the drawing represents. The smaller figure here is the son.

7. **MOTHER** Same as above, but here the figures are female.

8. **BABY** Papoose in cradleboard.

9. **I (ME, MY, MINE)**   The figure is pointing to himself.

10. **YOU (HE, HIS, HIM)**   The figure is pointing to someone else.

11. **WE (US, THEY)**

12. **MARRY**   TAKE (symbol 217) plus symbol for WOMAN.

13. **HUSBAND** Woman pointing to herself (My) plus symbol for MAN.

14. **WIFE** Man pointing to himself (My) plus symbol for WOMAN.

15. **OLD MAN (GRANDFATHER)** Also **OLD.** Represented by bent figure with cane.

16. **OLD WOMAN (GRANDMOTHER)** Also **OLD.** Same as above, but here the figure is female.

15

17. **ANCESTOR** Symbols for Father and Beyond (symbol 89) indicate the father beyond.

18. **WISE MAN (BRIGHT PERSON)** Also WISE. Lines radiating from the head are a sign of wisdom.

19. **MAN ALONE** Also ALONE. Within an enclosure, separated from the others. Break in circle is entrance to enclosure.

20. **HORSEMAN (RIDER)** Man on horse.

21. **SCOUT** The line below the figure represents the trail. The broken line indicates that he is keeping his eyes fixed on the trail. See symbol 209.

22. **NAME (TOTEM)** The name of this Indian is Morning Star. See symbols 194 and 205. To show other names, connect the appropriate symbols to an Indian head in the same way.

23. **SAME TRIBE** The two lines below the identical figures show that they come from the same group. Feathers around heads indicate same tribe.

24. **SAME CLAN** Here a totem is added to show that this drawing represents a clan, not a tribe. The drawing can also indicate **PATROL** or **CLUB**.

17

25. THIRTY PEOPLE The two outer lines are counted with each row. Any number of people can be shown in this way.

26. NINE WHITE MEN A white man is drawn with a stovepipe hat, because these hats were worn by 19th-century government officials. Each dot represents another man.

27. MIND The figure is touching his forehead.

28. CRAZY Curved lines coming from figure's head indicate that his mind is in a whirl.

29. **FIRE (FLAME, FLAMING)**

30. **CAMPFIRE**

31. **COUNCIL FIRE** The circle of short lines around the fire represents the people seated in council.

32. **INVITE (CALL TO COUNCIL)** COME (symbol 243) plus symbol for COUNCIL FIRE.

33. **TEPEE**

34. **CAMP (VILLAGE)** One tepee plus dots to indicate many more. To indicate **SOME** or **MANY** of any object, combine dots with its symbol.

35. **ARRIVE (RETURN)** Broken lines indicate footprints. The arrow shows that they are going toward the tepee.

36. **LEAVE (GO AWAY FROM)** Same as above, but here the arrow points away from the tepee.

37. **VISIT**   Indian with pipe (see symbol 70) enters tepee. Shaded top section of tepee indicates night visit. To indicate daytime visit, leave top section white.

38. **IN (AT) YOUR HOUSE**   White man enclosed within four walls.

39. **IN (AT) MY HOUSE**   Same as above, but here the figure is pointing to himself.

40. **WHITE MAN'S LOG HOUSE**   The tree alongside the house shows the house is made of logs.

41. **SCHOOLHOUSE (SCHOOL)** Lines radiating from the roof are a sign of wisdom, as in symbol 18.

42. **CHURCH**

43. **HOUSE (CABIN)**

44. **TOWN (VILLAGE, CITY)** One house plus dots to indicate many more.

45. HOSPITAL (MEDICINE HOUSE)
The wiggly lines above the hospital represent orenda (magic power).

46. MEDICINE TEPEE This tepee is like the white man's hospital. The radiating lines represent wisdom, and the totem shows what clan the tepee belongs to.

47. **MEDICINE (MEDICINE HERBS)**

48. **DRUGSTORE** Indicated by medicine herbs above the house.

23

49. **MEDICINE MAN (WITCH DOCTOR)** The wiggly lines above the Indian represent orenda.

50. **DOCTOR (WHITE MEDICINE MAN)** Same as symbol 49, but here the figure is a white man.

51. **LIFE** and **DEATH** The light circle represents life; the dark one represents death.

52. **SICK MAN** The figure is lying down, unable to get up.

53. SICK (SICKNESS) Did vour stomach ever feel like this?

54. COUGH (BAD COLD) Lines coming from mouth indicate coughing.

55. MEASLES

56. CHICKEN POX

57. HEAP (MANY, MUCH, PLENTY)
Represented by dots piled up in a mound.

58. **HUNGRY** The line across the body
indicates hunger pains.

59. **FAMINE (NO MEAT)** Empty meat
rack outside tepee.

60. **MEAT (ABUNDANCE, FOOD,
PLENTY OF FOOD)** Full meat rack.

61. GOING TO A FEAST Moccasin
tracks leading to a bowl of food.

62. EAT Represented by bowl of food
plus figure lifting hand to mouth.

63. DRINK Represented by water lines
plus figure lifting hand to mouth.

64. DRY The water lines are crossed
out to indicate no water. These cross-out
lines can be combined with other symbols
to indicate their opposites.

65. DANCE (DANCING) Figure is holding gourd rattle.

66. SING (SINGING, SONG) The curved lines coming from the mouth indicate the flow of the melody.

67. GREETING (GREETINGS) Hand extended.

68. LOVE The heart is within a magic circle.

69. **GUEST (VISITOR)** The seated figure is smoking, which is a sign of friendship.

70. **FRIENDSHIP** Also **WELCOME, PEACE.** A pipe is a sign of coming together in friendship.

71. **PEACE** You cannot shoot with a broken arrow.

72. **WAR** Arrows going in opposite directions. To indicate ARROW, draw only one.

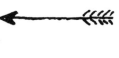

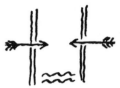

73. FIGHT ACROSS A RIVER The arrows aimed in opposite directions indicate war. The short wiggly lines always represent water, and here they represent the river.

74. SURPRISE ATTACK Tomahawks plunged into tepees indicate an attack on a sleeping village. The group of tepees represents the village.

75. CAPTIVES (PRISONERS) The two figures are tied together at the wrist.

76. COUNCIL WITH WHITE MAN The circle of short lines represents the people seated in council.

77. **TREATY**   Two Indians holding pipes. They are shown wearing different hair ornaments to indicate that they come from different tribes.

78. **ALLIES**   Also JOINED. A curved line connects the two figures.

79. **CHIEF (HEADMAN)**   The feather indicates rank.

80. **LEADER (COUNSELOR)**   "Carrying the pipe" is a symbol of leadership on a specific trip.

81. WAR BONNET

82. WAR FLAG (COUPSTICK) In war the greatest act of courage was to touch an enemy with a small wand or coupstick.

83. FLAG

84. AWARD (HONOR, COUP) Represented by an eagle feather.

85. **GOOD** and **BAD** Also ABOVE and BELOW. Good or above represented by black oval above the line; bad or below represented by black oval below the line.

and

86. **VERY BAD** Two ovals below the line against one above means that the bad outweighs the good. Two ovals above against one below means VERY GOOD.

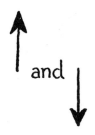

87. **AMONG** Shown by line curving among dots.

88. **UP** and **DOWN** Also HIGH and LOW. Arrows pointing up and down.

and

 **89. ACROSS** Also OVER, CROSS OVER, BEYOND. Arrow indicates the crossing from one side to the other.

90. CENTER (IN THE MIDDLE OF)

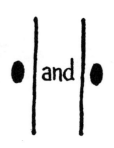 **91. BEFORE** and **AFTER** One oval is drawn before the line; the other oval is drawn after the line.

92. GRASS

93. **SPRING**   Short lines represent young grass.

94. **SUMMER**   Long lines represent full-grown grass.

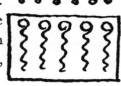

95. **AUTUMN (FALL)**   Indicated by falling leaves.

96. **WINTER (SNOW)**   Also **COLD.**
The dots represent snow. The square shows that everything is covered with snow. The wiggly lines represent shivers, showing how cold it is.

97. DEEP SNOW The snow is up to the man's waist.

98. CAMP IN DEEP SNOW Snow is piled around the tepee.

99. FLOOD Drawing of water lines rising above base of tepee.

100. RAIN The water lines are coming from the dome of the sky, represented by the arc.

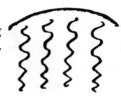

36

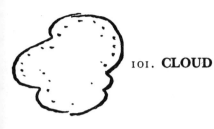 101. **CLOUD**

 102. **WIND**

 103. **CLEAR WEATHER** The arc represents a clear sky above the earth line.

104. **STORMY WEATHER (STORM)** Dark cloud in sky.

105. **LIGHTNING**

106. **EAST** A figure pointing to the left means East. To indicate WEST, the figure points to the right.

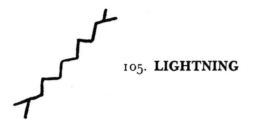

107. **LACROSSE** Represented by long-handled racket used in the game, with which the ball is caught, carried, or thrown.

108. **HOOP-AND-POLE GAME** Represented by hoop and pole. A hoop is rolled down a hill, and the men try to throw their poles through it as it passes.

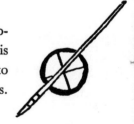

109. **PAWNEE INDIAN** Indicated by leg ornaments. These were made of Angora or feathers.

110. **NAVAHO INDIAN** Indicated by striped blanket.

111. **KIOWA INDIAN** Also CRAZY, STUPID. Hands waving at sides of head indicate "rattlebrains," the name given to the Kiowa Indians by the Sioux, who thought they were stupid.

112. **CHEYENNE INDIAN** Indicated by stripes on arm, which represent the striped arrow feathers the tribe used.

39

113. **MANDAN INDIAN** Indicated by hair style. These Indians cut their hair short and arranged it in this odd fashion.

114. **OMAHA INDIAN** Indicated by dark circles, which represent red paint these Indians used on their cheeks.

115. **HANDSOME (BEAUTIFUL)** Face plus symbol for GOOD.

116. **UGLY (HOMELY)** Face plus symbol for BAD.

117. **HUNT** Indicated by bow and arrow.

118. **GOOD HUNT** Bow and arrow plus symbol for GOOD.

119. **BAD HUNT** Bow and arrow plus symbol for BAD.

120. **CATCH (SNARE)** Also ROPE, LASSO. Drawing of lasso.

 121. **CAT**

122. **DOG**

 123. **BEAR**

124. **GRIZZLY BEAR** Same as above, but here big claws are added.

125. **DEAD BEAR** Drawn lying on its back. The eye is crossed out to show that it is closed. You can indicate that any animal is dead by drawing it this way.

126. **BEAVER** Indicated by the large flat tail.

127. **BEAVER IN ITS DEN** The break in the circle shows the entrance to the den. This symbol can be combined with other animals to indicate their dens.

128. **MOUNTAIN SHEEP**

129. **MOUSE**   Indicated by small ears and long tail.

130. **TURKEY**

131. **CROW**

132. **OWL**

 133. **EAGLE**

134. **THUNDERBIRD** A mythical bird supposed to cause thunder and lightning.

 135. **BUFFALO**

136. **COW**

 137. **DEER**

138. **DEER HUNT** The circle around the deer represents hunters. This symbol can be combined with other animals to indicate that they are being hunted.

 139. **WOLF**

140. **RABBIT**

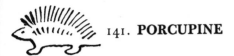 141. **PORCUPINE**

142. **RATTLESNAKE**

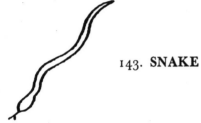 143. **SNAKE**

144. **FISH (FISHING)**

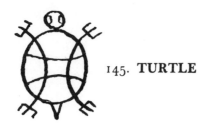

145. **TURTLE**

146. **FROG**

147. **HORSE**

148. **WHITE MAN'S HORSE** Indicated by horseshoe.

149. **INDIAN'S HORSE** Indicated by hoofprint. Indian horses weren't shod.

150. **CORRAL** Lines represent fence posts. Circles represent wire fencing.

151. **SADNESS (SORROW, SORRY)** His heart is on the ground.

152. **CRY** Tears flowing from the eyes plus water lines.

153. HAPPINESS (HAPPY PERSON)
His heart is where it belongs.

**154. GREAT SPIRIT EVERYWHERE
(GOD)** In the center and all about. The
triangles on the circle represent the four
points of the compass.

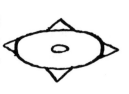

155. SPIRIT ABOVE Sky dome and
eye of Great Spirit.

156. PRAYER Hand reaching toward
the Great Spirit.

157. PRIEST (MINISTER, MISSION-ARY) The figure is wearing a black robe and carrying a cross.

158. GENEROUS (BIGHEARTED)

 **159. HONEST** Straight from the heart.

160. ALL (EVERYBODY) A circle to indicate taking in everything or everyone.

 161. **FLOWER**

162. **LEAF**

 163. **COUNTRY**   Grass and river.

164. **PLAINS (BUFFALO COUNTRY)**
Same as above plus buffalo heads.

 165. **CORN**

166. **LAKE**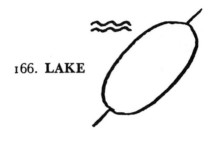

167. **HILL**

168. **PINE TREE**

169. **OLD TREE**   It is bent with age.

170. **FOREST**   One tree plus dots to indicate many more.

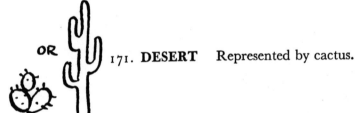

OR   171. **DESERT**   Represented by cactus.

172. **CANYON**   Indicated by narrow passage between two heights.

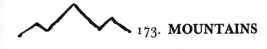 173. **MOUNTAINS**

174. **MOUNTAIN CLIMBING** Arrow indicates dotted lines are going up the mountain.

 175. **CAMP AT FOOT OF MOUN-TAINS** Arrow indicates dotted lines are going down the mountain. Campfire represents camp.

176. **DISCOVERY** Man holding up an object that he has just found.

177. **JANUARY** The snow moon. The moons (months) can be used to date letters.

178. **FEBRUARY** The hunger moon, indicated by a wolf so thin that its ribs show.

179. **MARCH** The crow moon.

180. **APRIL** The green-grass moon.

181. **MAY** The planting moon, indicated by a planting stick, used to make holes for seeds.

182. **JUNE** The wild-rose moon.

183. **JULY** The thunder moon.

184. **AUGUST** The green-corn moon.

185. **SEPTEMBER** The harvest moon.

186. **OCTOBER** The falling-leaf moon.

187. **NOVEMBER** The hunting moon.

188. **DECEMBER** The long-night moon.

189. DAY (TODAY) and **NIGHT (TO-NIGHT)** Sun and blackened sky dome.

190. THREE DAYS light circles.   Represented by

THREE NIGHTS dark circles.

THREE YEARS hanging circles.   Represented by

191. YESTERDAY Indicated by symbols for BEFORE and TODAY.

192. TOMORROW Indicated by symbols for AFTER and TODAY.

193. **TWO DAYS AND TWO NIGHTS**
Each day and night is indicated by a light and dark circle.

194. **SUNRISE (MORNING, EARLY)**

The arc represents the dome of the sky. The sun is in the East (left side of dome).

195. **NOON** The sun is directly overhead (center of dome).

196. **SUNSET (AFTERNOON, EVENING, LATE)** The sun is in the West (right side of dome).

III—⌖

IIII ⌖
IIII

197. THIRD DAY; EIGHTH DAY
The symbol for DAY plus lines to indicate how many. Used in dating letters, etc.

198. SUNDAY (MEDICINE DAY)
Symbol for DAY plus wiggly lines representing orenda (magical power).

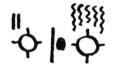

199. MONDAY One day after Sunday.

200. TUESDAY Two days after Sunday.

201. **WEDNESDAY**   Three   days   after Sunday.

202. **THURSDAY**   Three   days   before Sunday.

203. **FRIDAY**   Two days before Sunday.

204. **SATURDAY**   One day before Sun-day.

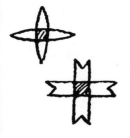

205. **STARS**

206. **MILKY WAY** Indians called this group of stars the wolf trail to the happy hunting grounds.

207. **CAMPING UNDER THE STARS (CAMP OUT)**

208. **BIRD TRACKS**

 **209. SEE (SAW, LOOKED)** Lines from eyes indicate sight.

210. HEAR (LISTEN) Sound lines coming from overlarge ears.

 **211. SLEEP** Figure on willow bed.

212. DREAM Dream lines rising from head of sleeping man.

213. ARISE   Going up in direction of arrow.

214. TRADE (SELL, EXCHANGE) One line crossing over another; exchanging positions with each other.

215. RICH (MANY HORSES) One horse plus dots to indicate many more. An Indian who owned many horses was rich.

216. POOR (NO HORSES) Symbol for HORSE plus cross-out lines.

217. **TAKE** Also CATCH. The figure is scooping something toward himself.

218. **GIVE (OFFER, BRING)** One figure is handing a gift to the other.

219. **HOLD** Indicated by hand grasping object.

220. **KILL (SLAY, HIT)** Man with tomahawk standing over figure.

221. **WALK (GO, WENT)**

222. **HIKE** Indicated by packs on backs of figures.

223. **LEAD (GO AHEAD OF)** Indicated by symbols for WALK and BEFORE.

224. **FOLLOW (GO BEHIND)** Indicated by symbols for WALK and AFTER.

225. GOOD ROAD (GOOD TRAIL)
Picture of road plus symbol for Good.

226. TRAIL and **MAIN ROAD**   Many
footprints indicate use by many people.

227. RIVER and **RIVER ISLAND**
Water lines in upper left corner. Double
wiggly lines in center represent winding
river. In right corner, river passing
around island (shaded area).

**228. CANOES ON RIVER (CANOE
TRIP)**   River with canoes on it, plus
water lines.

229. TRANSPORTATION Drawing of a travois, a primitive dog-drawn vehicle made of two trailing poles and a net or platform for the load. Used most often in moving camp.

230. REST These double lines are used in place of a period to indicate the end of a sentence.

231. QUESTION In sign language an Indian rotates his hand to indicate a question.

232. MONEY (WAMPUM) Indicated by section of a wampum belt.

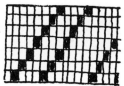

233. **BUFFALO ROBE**

234. **BLANKET** Also SLEEPING BAG.

235. **SWIM (SWIMMING)** Figure in water.

236. **MEET** Arrows coming together from opposite directions.

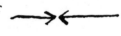

237. TALK (SPEAK) Indicated by lines coming from the mouth.

238. POWERFUL TALK The dots along the lines indicate emphasized words.

239. LIE Forked tongue indicates talking in two directions at once.

240. TRUTH Straight line coming from mouth indicates straight talk.

241. TALK TOGETHER (CONVER-SATION, POWWOW) Speech lines between two figures.

242. LETTER (NOTE, TALKING PAPER) Add dots to indicate **BOOK** (many pages).

243. COME The figure is beckoning to someone.

244. HARD Represented by a rock or a stone war-club head.

245. AUTOMOBILE Represented by drawing of automobile or steering wheel.

246. TRAIN

247. AIRPLANE

248. MOTION PICTURE (MOVIE) Indicated by camera.

3. *Index to Symbols and Their Key Numbers*

76

Answer in Key Numbers

					197	182

67   133

168 and 24   222   207   193   230   11   144

235   60   230   36   80   43   194   197   182

230   35   196   197   230

145

Answer in English

June 3

Greetings, Eagle:

The Pine Tree patrol will hike and camp out for three days and two nights. We will fish, swim, and have plenty of food. Will leave from the counselor's house on the morning of June 6. Will return on the evening of the 8th.

Turtle

Answer on Page 93

Answer on Page 94

85

Answer on Page 95

1959

Answer on Page 96

87

5. Exploit Markings

 SNOW DOTS Brave deed done by horse and rider in winter.

 HORSE HOOF MARKS Number of horses captured from enemy.

 EYE MARK Enables horse to see danger ahead.

 RED HAND Shows that wearer was struck by enemy.

 **LIGHTNING** Shows great speed.

 ESCAPE MARK Escape from enemy.

 **WOUND MARKS** Painted in red over scars and old wounds.

SLASH MARKS Coups (honors).

G.W.

6. The Cree Alphabet

The year was 1841. Within a small log cabin sat a tall, square-jawed man dressed in a good homespun suit and soft moose-hide moccasins. On the table in front of him was a square of birch bark, upon which he had scratched some odd-shaped figures with a sharp bone tool. The man was the Reverend James Evans, missionary to a band of Canadian Cree Indians.

Having learned the Cree's spoken language, Brother Black Robe, as the Indians called him, was taking their most commonly used syllables and giving them a written form. Later he visited Cree villages and followed the Indians to their fishing camps and wild-rice gatherings, teaching them the gospel by means of this new written language.

The syllabic alphabet Evans created is closer to our alphabet than to picture writing. The markings are angles and curves which represent certain sounds; they are not symbols for objects or actions. This syllabic writing is shown on page 91, but here it has been adapted to a letter alphabet.

After you have looked over the Cree alphabet symbols, it will be easy to translate this sentence.

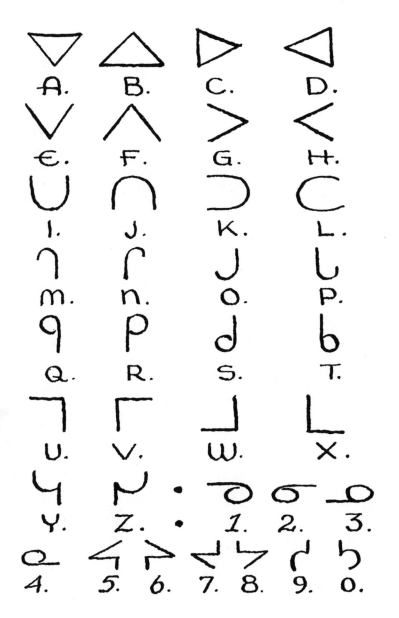

A. B. C. D.
E. F. G. H.
I. J. K. L.
m. n. o. p.
q. R. s. T.
U. V. W. X.
Y. Z. . 1. 2. 3.
4. 5. 6. 7. 8. 9. 0.

7. *Answers to Letters*

Answer in Key Numbers

67   126
236   9   91   41   197   181   39   230   110
221   209   248   29 and 72   230

134

Answer in English

Greetings, Beaver:

Meet me after school on May 3 at my house. We will go to see the movie "Flaming Arrow."

Thunderbird

Answer in Key Numbers

						197	188	
67	15							
9	151	210	10	53	230	192	9	243
45	209	10	230	9	218	242	230	50
85	218	10	47	10	54 and 64	230		
							135	

Answer in English

December 5

Greetings, Old Man:

I am sorry to hear that you are sick. Tomorrow I am coming to the hospital to see you. I will bring a book.

The doctor is good, and he will give you medicine to stop your cough.

Black Buffalo

94

Answer in Key Numbers

							197	185
67	165	161						
9	7	6	221	173	245	193	230	243
9	43	192	189	211	230	9	16	218
11	85	60	230	5	37	11	241	230
194	11	211	196	230				
							194	205

Answer in English

September 5

Greetings, Cornflower:

My mother and father are going to the mountains by automobile for two days and one night. Come to my house tomorrow night to sleep. My grandmother will give us good food. Friends will visit, and we will talk together. In the morning we will sleep late.

Morning Star

34   107

183   184

(spiral from left to center)   126   43   133   43   217

228   123   166   80   230   207   193   230

196   11   209   137   230   189   141   217

60   194   11   58   230   1   36   166   217

144   230   35 and 34   160   62   144   160   153

230

126   133

Answer in English

Camp Lacrosse

July   August

The Beaver cabin and the Eagle cabin took a canoe trip to Bear Lake with a counselor. Camped out for two days and two nights. In the afternoon they saw three deer. That night a porcupine took their food, and in the morning they were hungry. Two boys left for the lake, where they caught many fish. When they returned to the camp they all ate the fish, and everybody was happy.

Beaver   1959   Eagle

96